Walking the Black Dog

Elizabeth Lane

Walking the Black Dog

Walking the Black Dog
ISBN 978 1 74027 780 8
Copyright © Elizabeth Lane 2012

First published 2012
Reprinted 2014

Ginninderra Press
PO Box 3461 Port Adelaide SA 5015
www.ginninderrapress.com.au

Contents

Cleaning cutlery	7
Slipping	8
Walking the black dog	9
The institute of my mental state	10
The Calm	11
Toadstools	12
Hospital bed	13
Bonfire	14
Comforter	15
Hush	16
A Fine Madness	17
Cycle	18
Trying to Escape	19
Engulfed	20
Irritation	21
Shaken not stirred	22
Digging	23
Darkness descends	24
Electric Fence	25
Stone	26
The Great Grey Ocean	27
My black dog	28
Dear Doctor	29
Pills	30
Addiction	31
Vincent	32
An historical hero	33
A Broken Heart	34
That which lurks	35
A letter goodbye	36

The Suicide	37
Tropical House	38
A day in Morier	39
Weed	40
The actor's disappearance	41
Inheritance	42
To be enough	43
Impressions	44
The Wind	45
Electro-convulsive therapy	46
Wanting	47
Triviality	48
I wish	49
The End of War	50
The Shift	51
A Moment	52
The Front Gate	53
Moon Wish	54
Shoes	55
Maple Tree	56
The Natural	58

Cleaning cutlery

A large sharp blade
of a slicing knife
calls to me.
How easily
I could turn it
onto myself.
But the spoons
stop me
– the tiny teaspoons
with their dainty tails,
the soup spoons
with their round wise heads.
I would miss the tea
and the soup
and all the desserts
that come with the forks.

Slipping

I crawl out
from beneath my rock
and feel the sun
the warm rays
touch my heart
and it begins to beat again.
I take a step
and feel the muscles
in my legs
tense and flex.
I walk.
A gentle breeze
passes my flushed cheeks.
I start to run
I am galloping
gaining speed.
But then I lose control
I am hurtling along
everything is a blur.
I stumble
fall
lying flat on my face.
Slowly I get back up
take a step
trip
then slip
back down.
Here I will stay
until I regain my strength.

Walking the black dog

Wet black dog
slobber and silt
comes
bringing slurry
and smells of fish.
Panting and frothing
lunging and nuzzling
circles.
Covered in cobwebs
he wipes his dirty gob
on my clean white page.
Off again
investigating
sniffing in staccato
followed by a low rumble
growl
something's discovered.
Come black dog
heal.

The institute of my mental state

I could choose
to self-medicate
Be like you
Pretend
I am normal
Socially acceptable
Deny
I have a problem
Lost control
Suppress
my true thoughts
and feelings
Act along
Disguise
my pain
and fears
Feed into
delusion.
But like you tell me
I choose
depression
I choose
to live in it
face it
fight
I choose
to own it
embrace it
as mine
I choose
to wear it
The stigma.

The Calm

Low grey clouds creep
across the sky
hoping no one will notice.

Tree tops
of towering red gums
wave farewell to blue skies,

All birds are silent
livestock are tucked up
to keep in their heat.

A gentle wind
quietly begins to whistle
through trees.

Red, amber and golden leaves
flutter
to the ground.

Large rain drops
plop heavily, haphazardly
a prelude to showers.

The wind stops
all is still and silent
in waiting…

Toadstools

Golden-tipped
We grow huddled
In shadows

From dark rich soil
We silently emerge
Deceptively glowing

Beneath towering trees
We reach out
From their roots

We shine brightly
In contrast
To our pale cousin – but

We are not what we appear
Unpalatable, toxic
Inedible

Consuming just like the rest
But we are sick
With the poison

In a circle we gather
For protection
From the elements

Hospital bed

Lying in the fold-out hospital bed
after Isabelle broke her arm
anxiety was triggered.
There as a comfort for my child
I needed it more.
A short fall off the bed
led to an overnight stay,
in the paediatric ward,
which dragged on
hours
wreaking havoc
with my internal dialogue.
my eldest child
foolish antics
led to
theatre.
I kept a brave face
so did Isabelle
– but mine was a lie.

Bonfire

Twigs and leaves
dry and cracked,
lay cross-hatched
beneath dead branches
and hollow stumps
– ghosts of summers past.
Loose leaf matter
fuels the flame
but the thick sticks and logs
will keep the fire burning
through the cold winter night.

Comforter

Distracting me
from nagging thoughts
demanding nothing
a passive time waster.
Pacifying me,
numbing me
– from reality.
I sit mesmerised
engulfed in your glow.
You assist me
enable me
to avoid
– life.

Hush

Ripples of voices
Over and over.
Placing hands over ears
To block out noises –
the truth?
paranoia?
the questions
– keep out the voice
dictating
commanding
imposing
an alternate reality.

A Fine Madness

Brushed with flames
caressed by inferno
stolen many a great artist.
The artistic temperament
sensitive
delicate
fragile
Exquisite insanity
beneath the fiery exterior.

Cycle

Circling
inside my head
round and round
up and down.
Pedalling up hill
braking down.
Rapid rotation
of my mind
side to side
in and out
turning around
mixing up
spinning.

Trying to Escape

There is no escape
from their noise
squawking and screeching
bellows and taunts
following me
wherever I go.
Their voices echo
through the trees
above birds chorus
wind brushing
through bush.
Closing in on me
their sounds
drowning out
the calming calls of nature.

Engulfed

I step out of bed
into a sea of sludge
I try to wade through it
But it slowly
sucks me
deeper
deeper
deeper
into dark muddy depths
where I am powerless.
Exhausted
I lay
Engulfed.

Irritation

You constant annoyance
niggling, nagging
exasperating.
You continual nuisance
poking, prodding
harassing.
You ongoing aggravation
tugging, shoving
infuriating.
You eternal vexation
pushing, pulling
provoking.

Shaken not stirred

The puzzle pieces of my mind
have parted
I am agitated
– fragmented.
The coaxial cables
in my brain
have been disconnected.
My personas separated,
now warring.
I'm disjointed
frustrated
irritated
unsupported.

Digging

On hands and knees
I dig.
Scraping dirt
with my fingers
filling my nails
full of grit
Ferociously I scrabble
but deeper
darker
it gets.
Scooping soil
covered in filth
reaching out
clawing for escape
but down
I keep slipping.

Darkness descends

Darkness descends
A permanent night
With no moon in sight
I am submerged
In a sea of misery
I am walking against the flow
And I am alone in it.

Electric Fence

Grey afternoon sky
underlined by muddy paddocks
I trudge through the slop
to visit our horses.
Escaping house
its occupants
my toxic thoughts
– to clear my head.
I come across neighbour's electric fence
poisonous rumination returns.
I watch my hands reach out
vibration echoes
I'm knocked back
horses are startled.
I self administered
twelve volts of electric shock therapy
but I feel no better.

Stone

I am a cold
heavy, grey stone
motionless
colourless
solitary.
I sit alone
on the hard
unyielding ground.
I am a lifeless
lump of rock
untouched
unloved
I am a lonely object
wishing for the sun.

The Great Grey Ocean

The great grey ocean
creeps in
licks my toes
beckoning me.
The great grey ocean
rolls out
waving at me
to follow.
The great grey ocean
slides in
under my feet
and pulls at me.
The great grey ocean
floats out
calling me
to join it for eternity.

My black dog

Pulling the covers over my head
to block out the sunlight,
which has not warmed my insides
since the day you left.
My eyes well up without warning.
My heart beats double time,
maybe it is beating for us both.
If I leave this place,
our place,
invisible hands squeeze my throat
and I can't breathe.
My hands shake if I try to speak.
You would've steadied them
with your ears.
Doctor says, 'The stress is acute,'
but neither the blue nor the white tablets
will bring you back.
So here I am again
my black dog.

Dear Doctor

'It has been a particularly bad day.
I haven't felt this bad for a long time.
I feel detached.
Lethargic.
I can't keep momentum.
My head spins.
The ground beneath me feels unstable.
I'm crying continuously.
Can't leave the house.
I'm afraid of everything.
Doctor,
Can you help me?'

Pills

Purple pills
– white, green, blue
stick in my throat
make me drowsy
– till I pass out.
I am a walking pharmacy.

But the alternative?

fantasies of death
constant weeping
over analysing
followed by
oversensitivity
and severe irritability

The cost of my pills?

My quick mind sedated
Manual dexterity jittery.
A loss in the ability to do the things I love most.

Addiction

Poison calling
playtime.
Liquid attraction
powdered pleasures
luring.
An unreachable itch.
Time lost
sleepless, endless
days
nights.
highs
lows.
Mind scrambled
body battered.

Vincent

(Self-portrait with Bandaged Ear)

Past the bandages
to compress your severed ear
the pain painted in your eyes
speaks to me
about a hurting
beyond skin and bone.
Internal agony
radiates from your icy blue irises
Your inner suffering
called to you
and urged you
to cut off your own ear
and make your pain visible.

An historical hero

In the throes of mania
or with the Black Dog
at the foot of your sick bed
you made decisions that affected the world.
Self-medicating with whisky or scotch
you battled your private demons
while combating a public evil
– like history had never known.
You are a fine example of a hero
and a reminder
that we are all capable of achievement.
V is for victory.

A Broken Heart

You broke my heart
left it shattered
in tiny pieces.
I picked up the mess
and tried to put the pieces
back together again.
I held my heart together with sticky tape
but now
it doesn't beat the same.

That which lurks

Out of purple pills
and seven days till a doctor visit
the creature within
just below the skin
is stirring
begun creeping
scratching, clawing
to come out.
Seven days alone with this beast
could drive me
to desperate measures
to overpower it
and keep it at bay.

A letter goodbye

I love you.
I'm sorry
but I couldn't stay
the pain
was too great
too much
to endure.
I had to go.
What can I say
to make you understand
alleviate guilt
yours
mine.
Forgive me
if you can
I wanted to spare you
any more pain.

The Suicide

Sitting in the funeral parlour
surrounded by his family
his friends
all silently crying
I picture myself in the coffin
I see my family
my friends
my children
I see the pain it would cause
I feel that pain.
To take that final step
To end my suffering
would inflict more suffering
on more people.
I cry for the loss of this man
and I cry for the sorrow of others.

Tropical House

In a glass house
arms reach out covered in spikes.
The inhabitants are misplaced.
Tropical varieties
growing in an artificial setting
set amidst
Mediterranean climate.
Different species
grouped
in a see-through box
their only defence
their thorns.
Intangible
they are to be observed only.
Fed
watered
watched
but never touched.

A day in Morier

(the psychiatric ward)

Woken for breakfast at 8 a.m.
We eat quickly and quietly
Muttering simple pleasantries.
We all line up for medication
Served in a blue paper cup
With water.
At 9 we are called
For a morning meeting
The nurses tell us our schedule.
An outing from 9.30 till 11.
Lunch is delivered at 12.15.
We wait for a doctor's assessment at 1 p.m.
Then another outing from 2 till 4.
Dinner at 5.
Supper at 8
And night time medication
Served at 9.
Sedation
A stumble back to bed
To sleep
Until it all
Begins again
Tomorrow.

Weed

You are not conventionally beautiful
Your form and structure not as appealing
In comparison to the grace of those around you
You are ordinary, plain and overlooked
But you will outlast the glamour of their bloom
You will not wilt and fade against the elements
You will continue to grow and adapt to your environment
Long after their beauty withers.

The actor's disappearance

A bad review
that's all it took.
After failed attempt
at suicide
he fled
– on a boat.
Through sea spray
and thick grey fog
atmosphere mirroring
his mood.

Papers reported
his disappearance.
The play left
to go on with the show.

He returned
to hospital.
A cold bland room
expecting
his spirits to lift.
He recovered
re-emerged
his witty, articulate self
the facade of confidence
firmly fixed back in place.

Inheritance

I watch my children play
squealing, running
joyous
I wonder
the effect
impact
my shortcomings
are having on them.
Will they grow
to feel persecuted
angry
short-tempered
irritable, moody?
Will they snap
nit pick
worry incessantly
dislike themselves
wish to escape
the reality
they create?
Will I pass down this dreaded heirloom
that was passed
down to me?

To be enough

I want it with every
inch, nerve and drop of blood
to be enough
to feel enough
complete
whole.
I desire with all my senses
strength, urge and impulse
to be enough
to feel enough
acceptable
wanted.
I hope and wish
to be enough for you
but I crave more
to be enough for me.

Impressions

Impressions of a world
I composed in my mind
a painted picture
of myself
surrounded by you.

The Wind

Sat huddled
on the edge
I wait
for the wind
to move me.
Will I float up?
or rapidly descend
maybe I will blow left
or be pushed right.
Whichever way
the wind blows me
movement is imminent
and I will no longer
sit huddled
waiting for change.

Electro-convulsive therapy

The tiny electric impulses
administered to my head
jump started my heart
re-ignited my mind.
The small surge of energy
applied to my temple
have awakened me
from a deep dark slumber,
an endless sleep.
The little shocks of power
delivered to my brain
have shaken me
from the misery
I was consumed by.

Wanting

Wanting space
freedom
time
wanting company
understanding
acceptance
wanting music
beauty
art
wanting colour
light
shade
wanting satisfaction
contentment
happiness
wanting commitment
honesty
stability
wanting you
wanting me
wanting love.

Triviality

To put into words
that which nags
and bothers.
Trying to express
the many thoughts
and opinions.
Brooding over meaning
when my chain of thought
is broken.
Continually distracted…

Tattle tales and pointless questions
and squabbles over nothing.
Dirty hands
wiped on white T-shirts.
Big blue teary eyes
indicating the fast approaching wails.
Triviality will continue
until I give up my quest
and put down my pen.

I wish

I wish this feeling would go
It sits
in the pit of my stomach
and weighs heavy on my head.

I wish I could clear my mind
think straight
no worries, nagging thoughts
lingering guilt

I wish I could see the bright side
the sun
through clouds
the joy
the happiness.

I wish the sun would penetrate
my skin
reach my heart
warm my core.

I wish I was more tolerant
patient
comfortable in my own skin

I wish I could really believe
and see
how lucky I am.

The End of War

Both sides dropped weapons
walked to centre
the heart
the soul
and clasped each other's hands.
An understanding had been reached.
They'd been fighting
years
for the same outcome
peace.
But until now
they never realised
they were united.

The Shift

My mind has travelled
from the darkest corners
the deepest pits
into these brighter days.
My mind has journeyed
from shadow-lands
to warm sunny tomorrows.
My mind has discovered
a new horizon
a lush picture perfect place
where I can laugh
where I can dance
a place where I
can appreciate how good life is.

A Moment

Tomorrow never comes
and yesterday
has left
never to return.
All we have
is today
and each other.
We walk
through each moment
scared to look forward
and unable to look back.
We are inhabitants
of this second
trapped and free in one instant.
But we must take advantage
of it now
because it won't last.

The Front Gate

Towering red rusted steel
sharp arrows
pointing to sky.
They whine in pain
at each open.
Objects from another time.
Surrounded by shades of green
Overgrown scrub
Framed by two sandstone pillars,
rotting wooden paling
collapsing around them.
These giant gates stand guard
protecting
all my most precious possessions.

Moon Wish

I stare at a floating fingernail
against a black canvas
and wish
for forgiveness.
Hope
when the sun wakes
she will reach out to me
with the lengths
of her warm, slender arms
and grab me.
Shake me.
Wake me.
Break me
from hibernation.

Shoes

These old shoes
full of holes
stained from dirt
frayed laces
worn soles.

These old shoes
are travelled
garden
town.
Walked many miles
searching
coloured landscapes
– from grey.
Crossing boundaries
facing forks
finding home.

Maple Tree

Leaves of red
like the blood
pumping
through my veins
and behind my eyes.
Stars of fire.
Hands of anger.
Explosions of passion.

Winter comes, leaves fall
the tree is naked.
Its pale grey-white trunk
and thousand arms
reach for warmth.
A lonely figure.
A barren body.
A stripped soul.

Then when spring arrives
tiny buds of green emerge
Like shining emeralds.
bursting forth
fully formed.
Paint splashes of jade
children's handprints
on blue skies.
Summer finally comes
the leaves have matured.
Their browning edges
curl in comfort
from the ardour of the sun.
Blowing lazily,
savouring every moment
of their golden days.

The Natural

She walks her way
making exact impressions
every step
every stroke

She is accepting
of nature
of all people
their difference

She is strong
carrying weighty ideas
problems and solutions
which she can vocalise

She is at peace
with where she is
what she's doing
who she is.

www.ingramcontent.com/pod-product-compliance
Lightning Source LLC
Chambersburg PA
CBHW062203100526
44589CB00014B/1924